...If You Were a PIONEER on the Prairie

by Anne Kamma
Illustrated by James Watling

SCHOLASTIC INC.

New York   Toronto   London   Auckland   Sydney
Mexico City   New Delhi   Hong Kong   Buenos Aires

ISBN 0-439-41428-8

12 11 10 9 8 7 6   5 6 7 8/0

Printed in the U.S.A.
First printing, March 2003

Art direction by Jennifer Rinaldi
Book design by Christopher A. Motil

For Lise and Els and Sarah, who are also pioneers

ACKNOWLEDGMENTS

With grateful thanks to the many helpful people at the U.S. Forest Service, National Parks Service, the Nature Conservancy, the Grasslands National Park of Canada, and the Nebraska State Historical Society; Ellen Levine; Frank J. Popper, Rutgers University; Rick Ewig, University of Wyoming; my editor, Eva Moore; Susan Gordis; Inger Koedt; Bonnie Kreps; Fran Manushkin; Sam Seuratt; Toby Yuen; Kay Crank and Margaret Waterson, Battenkill Books, Cambridge, New York. The bug song is reprinted from Roger L. Welsch's *Sod Walls: The Story of the Nebraska Sod House* (Broken Bow, Nebraska: Purcells, Inc., 1968). Grace Snyder's quotes are from her wonderful book, *No Time on My Hands* (Caldwell, Idaho: The Caxton Printers, Ltd., 1963).

🌾🌾 CONTENTS 🌾🌾

Introduction

The first pioneers who traveled west weren't going to the prairie. They were going to Oregon and California. But they had to cross the prairie to get there.

As they traveled in covered wagons, all they saw was grass, grass, and more grass. The prairie had almost no trees and very little water. As they got farther west, the prairie got drier — so dry, in fact, that it was called the Great American Desert on their maps. The pioneers didn't think anyone except the Indians could live in such a place.

But all that changed after gold was discovered in California in 1848. Suddenly, more people than ever were rushing west, hoping to strike it rich. Special stores called road ranches sprang up on the prairie along the busy wagon trails. They served hot meals, sold supplies, and cared for the tired oxen and horses that pulled the covered wagons. Road ranchers raised their own cattle and often grew their own vegetables. People began to notice that you could actually live on this land. Word spread, and soon pioneers were living all over the prairie.

CANADA

UNITED STATES

*The western part
of the prairie is
also called the
Great Plains.*

MEXICO

When did pioneers live on the prairie? The colored part of the time line shows you.

1776	1803	1835	1848	1861–1865	1869	1879	1890	1900
The 13 American colonies declare independence from England	The U.S. buys most of the prairie land in the Louisiana Purchase	First pioneers go west on the Oregon Trail	Gold discovered in California	The Civil War — President Lincoln signs Homestead Act (1862)	Railroad across the U.S. completed	Thomas Edison invents electric lightbulb	Most of the prairie land settled	Early automobiles appear in the U.S.

What was the prairie like?

Just imagine — only 150 years ago, America had the greatest grasslands the earth has ever seen.

The wind blew the grass in endless waves across the prairie. You could walk for miles and miles and never see a tree, except for those growing along the rivers. The grass and the sky seemed to go on forever. Pioneers called it a sea of grass.

Winters were freezing cold, with blizzards of ice dust sweeping down from the Arctic. Summers were very hot and dry, with freak hailstorms and tornadoes. As the grass

dried, prairie fires swept across the open land. Indians had lived on the prairie for thousands of years. Some who lived along the rivers, like the Pawnee, were both farmers and hunters. Others, like the Lakota Sioux, were mainly hunters.

More than sixty million buffalo roamed the prairie. When they ran, the earth shook. There were also antelope, wolves, bears, prairie dogs, and millions of rattlesnakes. As the weather warmed, the air filled with songbirds and butterflies.

Why did people want to come to the prairie?

In 1803, the United States bought most of the prairie from France as part of the Louisiana Purchase. With all this new land, people thought the government should give it away free.

That's what President Abraham Lincoln thought, too. So in 1862, he signed the Homestead Act. Now anyone could get 160 acres free if he was willing to farm it. Even foreigners could get free land, as long as they promised to become citizens.

People talked about all the wonderful things they could do if they moved west to the prairie. They could own their own farms. They could start a store or other business in a

Rocky Mts.

Mississippi River

Atlantic Ocean

When the United States became a new nation in 1783, it was much smaller than it is today. U.S. territory went only from the Atlantic Ocean to the Mississippi River. The land west of the Mississippi was claimed by Spain, which later sold it to France.

In 1803, the United States bought the land between the Mississippi River and the Rocky Mountains from France for $15 million. It was called the Louisiana Purchase, and it made the United States twice as big. Most of this new land was prairie.

brand-new town. Maybe they could even start a new town! Maybe they'd become rich or famous!

Some of the people who moved to the prairie were soldiers who had fought in the Civil War and wanted a new place to start over. Others were African-Americans who had been slaves before the war and wanted to find a place of their own. Farmers who had struggled to make a living in the East came. Poor families and religious groups came. The Irish, Germans, and Scandinavians came. All wanted a chance to make a new life on the great, wild prairie.

How did people learn about the prairie?

Each new town wanted pioneers to come to their town — either to buy town land or to settle nearby. So the town owners printed up a lot of information to advertise their towns. Some towns even hired agents to stand at riverboat landings when the pioneers arrived and hand out advertisement fliers.

The advertisements had drawings of beautiful towns. Sometimes, though, those beautiful towns didn't really exist! In those early days, many families arrived at a place only to find that the "town" was nothing but a few shacks, a store, and a lot of prairie dogs.

Railroad companies were big advertisers. The U.S. government had given them more than 150 million acres of free land as "payment" for building a railroad across America. Most of this land was very valuable because it lay next to the railroad tracks. The railroads wanted to sell the land, so they advertised in the East and in Europe. The railroads wanted pioneers to come to the prairie even if they *didn't* buy land. The more pioneers living there, the more customers the railroads had, and the more money they made!

How would you get to the prairie?

Some families traveled in covered wagons. That way they could bring many things with them — even furniture and plows. Your family might even travel in two wagons.

A covered wagon was like a little home on wheels. All day the horses or oxen pulled the wagon along. Sometimes you'd ride, sometimes you'd walk. In the evenings, your family set up camp, and you'd help your mother cook the meals. At night, you'd crawl under your warm blanket and go to sleep in the wagon.

Could you go by train or boat?

Yes. Every year the railroads built tracks farther and farther into the wild prairie. So if your new home was near a train station, you might go by train if your family could afford it.

Trains were much slower then. Rides were bumpy, and sometimes black smoke and ashes flew in the window and got all over your face and clothing. But nobody minded that much, because trains were the fastest and easiest way to go.

Traveling by riverboat was a lot of fun. There'd be bands playing tunes like "Oh, Susannah," and lots of delicious food to eat. Many passengers became friends during the long trip. One group decided to settle together when they got to Nebraska. They named their new town Beatrice, after one of their daughters.

Riverboats took you only part of the way, though. You'd have to take a stagecoach or wagon to your homestead.

How would you build your house?

There were almost no trees on the prairie. So most pioneers built their houses out of grass and dirt. The deep roots of the prairie grass hold the soil tightly together. This is called sod. The pioneers cut up sod to make "bricks."

Here's how they did it. First they plowed a long strip of prairie grass and cut it into three-foot-long bricks. Then they stacked the sod bricks on top of one another to make thick walls. You had to plow almost an acre of land to get enough bricks for a sod house.

Door frames and window frames were made of wood, but the pioneers often used buffalo robes for doors. If glass was too expensive, people covered their windows with oiled paper or animal skins.

The roof was made of — you guessed it — more sod! Strong wooden beams and branches held up the roof. With help from a neighbor, it took almost a week to build a sod house.

There were no toilets inside the house. The pioneers used outhouses instead. Outhouses, animal pens, and barns were often made of sod, too.

Sod was very important — without it, most pioneers would not have been able to build their houses and settle the prairie.

Did any pioneers live in wooden houses?

Yes, some did. If there were trees growing nearby, pioneers might chop them down and build wooden log houses. But chances are they wouldn't find any trees, unless they lived near rivers or streams.

They might also live in wooden houses if they had enough money to buy wooden boards.

Would you live in a dugout?

You might. Many pioneer families started out in a dugout until they could make a better place to live. Dugouts were smaller and not as comfortable as sod houses.

A dugout was a house dug out of the side of a riverbank or hill. It took only a few days to make. The front part was closed off with sod bricks and had a door and window.

A stovepipe chimney stuck up through the hill, which was actually the roof of the house. When you stood on the roof, it was sometimes hard to see that there was a house underneath.

One girl sleeping in a dugout was awakened one night by a terrible crash and a moo. Her mother lit a candle, and there in the middle of the room stood their cow, Tillie. She had been grazing on the roof and had fallen through!

Would you get dirty living in a sod house?

Yes! Dirt was always falling off the walls and ceiling. It got in your hair, your clothes, and your bed. But the pioneers had a few tricks for keeping out the dirt. Some families plastered their walls with clay. When the clay hardened, it made nice smooth walls. Others covered their walls with newspapers.

Even your floor was probably made of dirt, because wood was very expensive. You could cover the floor with fresh hay. If your family had saved up enough rags, you could make a rag carpet, which was put down right on top of the hay.

Once you had clay walls and a carpet on the floor, you'd start looking and feeling a lot cleaner.

If it rained a lot, though, you had trouble. Muddy water leaked through the ceiling — and it could keep dripping for three days after the rain stopped! You had to put pots everywhere to catch the drips.

Was your house crowded?

Yes, it could be very crowded. Many families had five or six children, and sod houses were small.

It was most crowded at bedtime. First you had to move the table and some chairs outside to make sleeping room. There was probably only one bed. Everyone who couldn't fit in the bed had to sleep on the floor. They slept on furry buffalo skins or on mattresses filled with hay. Babies often slept in wooden boxes.

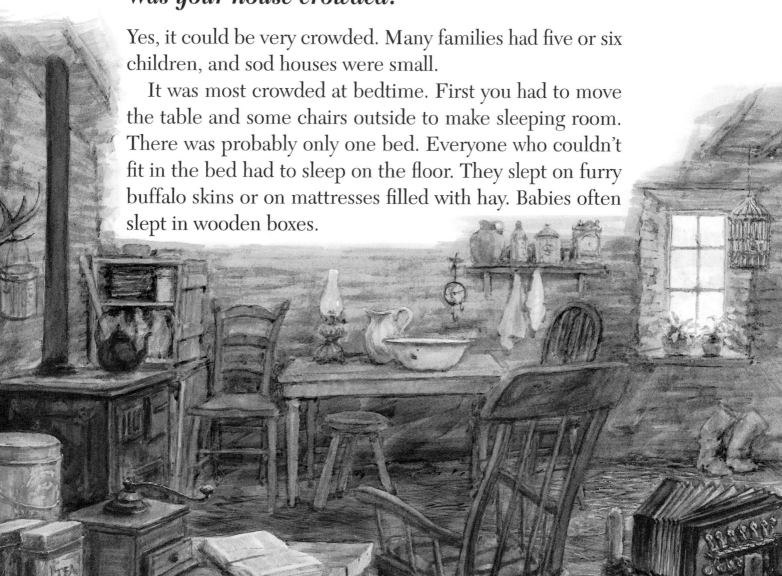

The pioneers were always ready to help one another, and they loved having visitors. So if a stranger or traveling preacher stopped by, he was invited to stay over. One boy remembered when the circus strongman (who juggled cannonballs), the bareback rider, and the fat boy weighing 300 pounds all stayed overnight in his house.

What would you really hate about living in a sod house?

There were fleas everywhere — in your house, your yard, the grass. The prairie was crawling with them. Since everybody was scratching, it was considered good manners to scratch yourself.

There were lots of bedbugs, too. They came out at night and bit you while you slept. The women and girls would have to drag the bedding out into the sun and pick off every bug. Inside, they went over cracks in the walls and furniture with chicken feathers dipped in kerosene. That killed off the bedbugs.

Worst of all, though, were the snakes — especially the rattlesnakes. You never knew when one would crawl through the walls or roof. Sometimes you'd look up and see a snake poking its head through the ceiling, watching you. People hung sheets over their beds to keep snakes from falling on them while they were asleep.

The people learned to laugh at their problems.
They made up funny little songs, like this one:

How happy I feel when I crawl into bed,
And a rattlesnake rattles a tune at my head.
And the gay little centipede void of all fear
Crawls over my neck and down into my ear.
And the gay little bedbugs so cheerful and bright,
They keep me a-laughing two-thirds of the night.
And the gay little flea with sharp tacks on his toes
Plays "Why don't you catch me" all over my nose.

How would you heat your house?

With buffalo droppings! The pioneers called them buffalo
chips. They were burned in a stove, like wood. It was the
children's job to help pick them up.

You'd go out into the prairie where herds of buffalo had
been grazing. After packing your sack full of hard, dried
buffalo chips, you'd bring them home and stack them next
to the house.

Now, you might think that buffalo chips had a terrible smell, but they didn't. They smelled like the grass the buffalo ate. The chips made a hot, clean fire, so you could use them in your stove for cooking. You could also use cow chips, corncobs, cornstalks, and hay.

The pioneers *hated* using hay, because it burned so quickly. To keep a good fire going, you had to stand by the stove all the time and put in more hay. It was a hot and boring job. But it was hay that sometimes saved a family from freezing to death during a blizzard.

What were some special pioneer tricks?

The early pioneers were too poor to buy most things. They used all kinds of tricks for making things themselves.

- Corncobs made handy toothbrushes, with salt as toothpaste.
- A bunch of prairie grasses tied together made a broom.
- Skunk oil was sometimes used for oil lamps.
- Flour sacks were made into curtains or clothes.
- A bucket of water was your "mirror."
- Wooden boxes became chairs and cupboards.
- Buffalo bones were ground up and fed to the chickens.
- Braided straw was used to make shoes.
- Burned cornmeal and molasses made "coffee."

And one teacher who needed a globe for her students made one by painting the world on an egg!

How did the pioneers keep food from spoiling?

The pioneers had no refrigerators or freezers, but they had many other ways to keep food from spoiling.

The coolest place on the farm was the well. That's where they kept food like milk and butter. They just put it in a bucket and lowered it down by rope into the cool air below.

Another cool place to put food was the cellar. The cellar wasn't underneath the house. It was a small room dug into the ground, with its own sod roof and wooden door.

The pioneers also made food last longer by drying, salting, preserving, or pickling it.

It was usually the children's job to cut up the vegetables and put them out to dry in the hot prairie air. The trick was to cut the vegetables into small, thin pieces. Otherwise the vegetables rotted before they had a chance to dry out.

Cucumbers and cabbage were soaked in vinegar and water in big wooden barrels and stored in the cellar next to barrels of salted meat. In the summer, children picked wild plums and berries, which were dried or made into delicious sweet jellies for the long winter ahead.

What would you wear?

The early pioneers wore plain clothes, like those in this picture. If you wore fancy clothes, people thought you were stuck-up.

Sometimes when your clothes wore out, there wasn't any money to buy new ones. Then your mother would sew you a shirt or dress out of flour sacks or woolen army blankets.

Women and girls weren't supposed to wear pants in those days, even when they went horseback riding. But some girls growing up on the prairie had different ideas. Grace Snyder remembers how thrilled she was when her mother finally made her a pair of denim pants with a matching jacket.

Most people wore boots. But if your boots got wet, you were in big trouble. That's because the leather shrank when it dried out, so your boots ended up a size too small! You'd still have to put those boots back on in the morning, though. Sometimes your mother had to put soap on your feet to force them into the boots. Once you got them on, it took a few hours of miserable pain before the boots finally stretched back to their right size again.

Everybody loved spring. Then you could go barefoot and feel the soft new prairie grass beneath your feet. Even adults went barefoot much of the time. If you went to church, you carried your shoes under your arm and put them on right before you walked in the door.

What would you eat?

Corn — at almost every meal! The pioneers didn't have very much money, but they did have plenty of corn. They grew it themselves by the wagonloads. In fact, most of what you ate came from your own farm. So you'd eat a lot of corn bread and corn mush. Pancakes and puddings were made out of cornmeal, too. You'd pour molasses, which is a kind of syrup, on top. White flour was so expensive, biscuits made with white flour were served for special desserts.

People got really tired of eating corn bread every day. Some children hated corn bread so much that they refused to eat it when they grew up.

In the summer, you'd eat beans, squash, potatoes, and other vegetables from the garden you had helped your mother grow. Big, delicious watermelons, too.

When the pioneers first came to the prairie, there were buffalo, deer, and antelope to hunt. That's how your family got some of its fresh meat. After a while these animals were gone, but you could still hunt prairie chickens and rabbits. You might also raise chickens, pigs, or turkeys to eat. Much of the time, though, you'd eat salt pork.

Where would you get water?

The first settlers spent hours each day hauling water from nearby streams. You might even have to travel miles by wagon to get water. But there was one place on the prairie where there was lots and lots of water — under your feet, deep down in the ground! The prairie sat on top of huge underground lakes, called aquifers.

To reach this underground water you had to dig a deep well — sometimes 300 feet down. Most people dug their own wells. Digging wells was dangerous. Sometimes the walls caved in. And many were killed by a deadly gas that can collect in the bottom of wells.

Once you had a well next to your house, though, you didn't have to carry water very far.

What were windmills used for?

Pumping well water by hand took a long time. But a Connecticut mechanic named Daniel Halladay had an idea: Why not let the wind do the pumping! So he invented a special kind of windmill to do just that. The windmill pumped water steadily, twenty-four hours a day.

The railroad companies were the first to use Halladay's windmills. They needed water for their locomotives and for the workers who were building the new tracks across the wild prairie.

Pioneers raising cattle were the next to use windmills. Now they could graze their cattle on land that had no rivers or streams — all they had to do was dig a well and put up a windmill. The water was pumped into big containers, so the cattle could drink whenever they wanted to. Pretty soon pioneer families wanted windmills to pump their water for them.

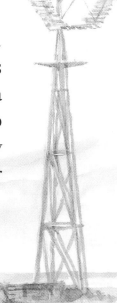

Would you get lonely?

You might. People lived miles away from one another. You could go for weeks and see only your own family.

The prairie also felt lonely to some people because there were so few trees — just endless grass and wind.

So what did people do? They had parties! Sometimes a family piled into a wagon at the end of a workday and drove to their neighbor's house for a surprise visit.

Once in a while, on Sundays, you got to play with children on nearby farms. Your family would bring food along for the trip and stay all day, visiting.

The pioneers were always helping one another at harvest time and at "bees." At bees, you got together to do something special — maybe build a school or church. Bees were fun, because when the work was done, you ate a delicious supper and danced long into the night. Everyone joined in — kids and old people, too.

Of course, as more people moved to the prairie, you'd feel less lonely.

Did the pioneers and the Indians get along?

At first, many of the pioneers traded with the Indians. A few even became friendly with their Indian neighbors. One group of Indians became so friendly with a group of German pioneers that they learned to speak German.

The U.S. government had promised that land west of the Missouri River would belong to the Indians forever. But the government broke the treaties it had signed with the Indians. Often, Indians were attacked and killed. Little by little, as land-hungry pioneers pushed farther west, the Indians lost their land.

The Indians fought against the U.S. soldiers and sometimes attacked the pioneers. But in the end, the Indians couldn't win. There were too many soldiers and too many settlers. By 1890, all the tribes had been forced onto Indian reservations.

Was the prairie good for farming?

Yes, the soil was rich and fertile. And there weren't any rocks or trees to be cleared away.

But there was one big problem. The iron plows in those days weren't sharp enough to cut through the thick, matted roots of the prairie grass. The plows bent out of shape whenever the farmers tried to use them. If it hadn't been for a man named John Deere, the pioneers might all have had to go back home.

John Deere was a blacksmith. He invented a new steel plow with a hard, sharp blade. Finally, the farmers had a plow that could turn the grasslands into fields ready to be planted.

Why were farmers afraid of grasshoppers?

Imagine this: It's a warm summer day. Suddenly, you look up and see a strange dark cloud coming toward you. It is huge — more than a hundred miles wide — and moving very fast. It's making a roaring, buzzing sound and blocking out the sun. Then grasshoppers start falling out of the sky, millions of them. They crawl under your clothes and down your neck. They gobble up everything — the corn, wheat, vegetables, even your clothing and window curtains. Your mother runs out and covers the vegetable garden with blankets, but the hoppers eat right through them, too. No matter how many you kill, more keep on coming.

They stay for a few days. Then they leave, riding the wind. You look around you. The corn and wheat are completely gone. Vegetables, too. There is nothing left growing for your family to sell or eat.

Fortunately, the grasshoppers didn't come often, but when they did, whole communities were made poor.

Could you get lost on the prairie?

Yes, it was easy to get lost because there were so few trees and houses. You could walk for miles and everything would look the same as when you started.

The pioneers came up with all sorts of ways to help find their way. Sometimes they marked the way to town by putting poles in the grass along the way. Another trick was to tie rags to tall weeds.

It was especially dangerous to get lost in the tall grass that grew on the eastern prairie. This grass could be eight feet high — so high that even a tall man couldn't see over the top. Once in a while, children who were lost died.

In 1868, two girls, seven and eight years old, got lost while walking out to see their brother, who was herding cattle. The parents searched for days and finally concluded the girls were dead. Not long after, the father found them by accident, asleep in the tall grass. He had to carry them home because they were too weak to walk.

What did boys have to learn?

Men did most of the farmwork, so if you were a boy, that's what you'd have to learn.

One of the hardest jobs was plowing the tough prairie grass to make a new field. It usually took six strong oxen to pull the plow. One man guided the plow, while a second man often sat on top of the plow to keep the blade from popping out of the ground. You shouted "Haw!" if you wanted the oxen to turn left, "Gee!" to turn them right, and "Whoa!" to make them stop.

Boys also learned how to work farm machinery, like the threshing and hay-cutting machines — all pulled by horses or oxen.

Building houses and barns and repairing tools were the men's jobs, so you'd learn those, too.

What did girls have to learn?

It was the women's job to make the soap and candles and to sew everyone's clothes. So if you were a girl, that's what you'd learn.

To make soap, you put scraps of animal fat into a big pot. Then you added lye, which is water that has dripped through ashes. After boiling this for a few hours, you'd have a slippery, jellylike soap called soft soap. This is what pioneer women used for cleaning just about everything.

You'd also learn how to cook on a cookstove. The midday meal was the biggest meal of the day — especially at harvest time, when there might be hired men to feed, too. When you rang the bell, they'd all rush in from the fields. You'd serve lots of fried chicken, mashed potatoes, gravy, corn bread, butter, and pies. If the hired men didn't like the food, they might not come back next year, so it was important to be a good cook.

Girls also did farmwork — especially if they didn't have any brothers. One girl kept a diary in 1865. Here is a list of what she did during the year: She worked in the vegetable garden, herded cattle, hunted, picked corn, stacked the cut wheat, drove the horses for haying, stripped the leaves off the sugarcanes, picked fruit, carried fuel, cut oats, and dug up potatoes.

Would you have fun?

There was plenty of time for fun. Kids played group games like dog-and-deer. And everybody on the prairie played baseball, including the girls.

You made your own baseball by winding yarn from an old sock into a ball, then covering it with leather from an old boot. Gloves and protectors weren't used, just a ball and bat.

The Fourth of July and the county fair were great celebrations. But the most exciting was the circus. Even before you saw the long line of circus wagons coming across the open prairie, an advance man had put up posters. W. Coe's Circus advertised "Elephants, Giants, Sea Monsters, and Trick Ponies!" Another circus might advertise a chariot race, acrobats, knights in armor, and wild tigers.

Admission was often fifty cents for children and seventy-five cents for adults. Nobody wanted to miss the circus, even if the family had to drive half the day to get there.

Mostly, though, the pioneers had to make their own fun. In the winter, the "literaries" drew a good crowd. Anyone could stand up and perform. You might read a poem or sing a song. One evening, Grace Snyder and her sister Florry sang all the verses of "The Drunkard's Lone Child." But it was a first grader named Leonard Maline who got the most applause, and laughs, with:

> *Times are hard an' girls are plenty,*
> *So don't get married till yer twenty.*

Would you have a pet?

Yes, you'd probably have a dog. Most pioneers did. Dogs were part of the family. They protected you against wild animals, like wolves, and helped with hunting and cattle herding. When Laura Ingalls's whole family lay sick with malaria, it was their bulldog, Jack, that went for help. Jack found Doctor Tan and led him back to the Ingalls cabin.

Or you might have a wild pet. One family brought home a young antelope that had been injured. Pretty soon it was well and running around the farm. The antelope was shy with strangers, but very tame with the family, and the children loved it.

Grace Snyder took her pet rooster along for company when she was out alone herding the family's cattle. After the little white rooster had stuffed himself on grasshoppers, he'd sit down next to her, clucking and chirping so long as she answered him back.

What was a prairie fire like?

Nothing frightened the pioneers more than a prairie fire. It came roaring across the dry prairie, burning everything in front of it. Sometimes the wall of fire was miles wide. You couldn't outrun it, even on the fastest horse.

The only way to survive was to find a place without any dry grass. If you were near a river, you ran there. If you were near a plowed field, you ran and sat in the middle of it. If you lived in a sod house, you ran inside. One woman saved herself and her child by crawling into the well.

Everyone stopped what they were doing and rushed to help if they saw a prairie fire coming. If there was time, they plowed a strip of land, called a firebreak, around the endangered farms. If there was wheat or corn growing in the fields, they'd try to plow firebreaks around them, too.

You couldn't fight the front of the fire, but you could sometimes fight it on the sides. People grabbed wet blankets or whatever they could find and started beating out the fire. Sometimes men on horseback tied ropes to the blankets and rode back and forth as fast as they could, dragging the blankets over the fire to smother it. After hours of fire fighting, people were covered with black soot. But many times they saved their neighbor's farm — or their own.

Where would you buy things?

Of course you could buy things in town. But sometimes the "store" came to you! Traveling peddlers arrived in horse-drawn wagons or walked, carrying everything on their backs.

The peddlers stopped at your house and tried to sell you something — a new shirt, or a book, or needles and thread. Some sold medicines, some sold eyeglasses. There was no eye examination. You tried on different glasses until you found a pair that helped you see better. The jewelry peddler was very popular because he repaired clocks, which sometimes had been broken for weeks.

Starting in the 1870s, you could also shop by mail. Sears, Roebuck and Montgomery Ward catalogs sold things you couldn't buy in town or from peddlers — like beautiful furniture and prairie stoves that burned corncobs.

How would you earn money?

It wasn't easy to make money when the pioneers first came to the prairie.

Your father might have to go away for a few months and work for the railroad. He'd leave after the harvest was done. The rest of the family took care of the farm while he was gone. You were lucky if your father found a construction job in a nearby town instead.

Children earned money for their families, too. One way was to sell eggs. You'd help your mother raise the chickens and gather the eggs. The egg money you got was saved to buy leather shoes, salt, and other important things your family couldn't make themselves.

In the winter, you could collect buffalo bones. So many buffalo had been killed by the buffalo hunters that millions of bones lay scattered all over the prairie. Factories in the East bought these bones to make phosphates and carbon. Gathering up the bones was cold, hard work, and it paid less than a dollar a day. But it was sometimes the only way for your family to earn money. One company bought six million buffalo skeletons in seven years.

Sometimes pioneers didn't even use money. When they needed something, they traded with one another instead.

One woman wanted to plant potatoes. So she traded some of her eggs for seed potatoes. Another woman traded her beautiful wedding bonnet for a female pig that she bred for many years. This pig was the beginning of hundreds of pigs she raised.

You could also trade your work. One woman washed laundry in exchange for a loaf of wheat bread.

Would you go to town?

Going to town was a big adventure, and sometimes the whole family went along. You had to bring bedding and food for the trip, because you might be gone a week. If your mother was bringing eggs to sell or trade, you'd pack them in pails of oats to keep the eggs from breaking.

As you drove your wagon across the prairie, you'd stop to ask your neighbors if they needed anything in town.

Early pioneer towns didn't smell very good. Pigs and chickens ran around loose, and there were horse droppings everywhere. When it rained, you had to cross the muddy street on special stepping-stones.

The first place you headed for was the general store. One pioneer girl remembered the store's fine smell of dried fruit, vinegar, strong cheese, shoe leather, smoked ham, dill pickles in open barrels, new cloth, molasses, fresh-cut plug tobacco, and a hundred other things.

After the eggs were sold or traded, your parents stocked up on salt, beans, salt pork, and other things needed for the coming winter. Leftover money went to buy new shoes and clothes — and, if you were lucky, some delicious penny candies to suck on while you made the long trip home.

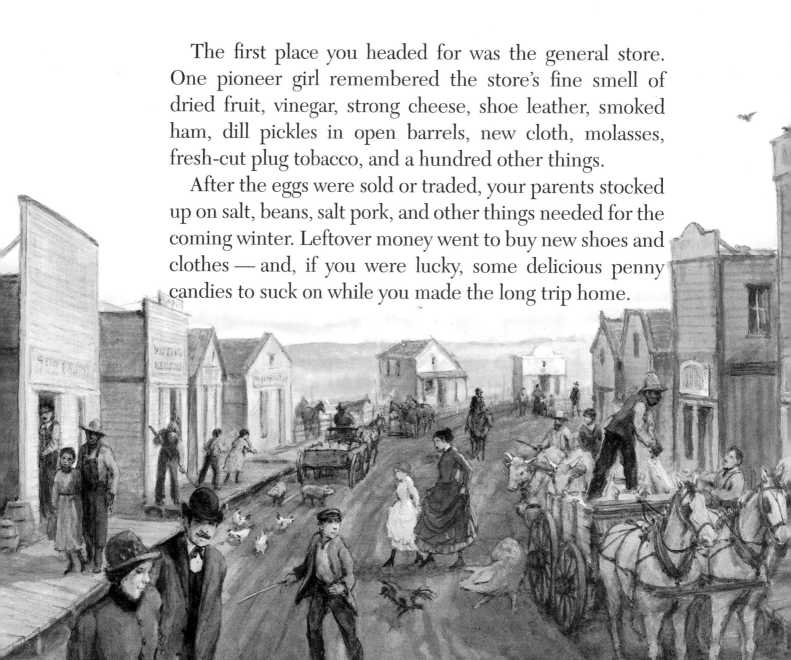

When did really strange things happen?

Some very strange things happened when tornadoes swept through. In 1854, Ely Moore was out buffalo hunting with some Indian friends when they saw a tornado coming toward them. The huge funnel cloud was sucking up everything in its path. But the funnel skipped right over the hunters, so they survived. After the storm, they went to look at the spot where the funnel had touched down again. Miles of grass had been stripped from the ground, leaving bare dirt. Two large buffalo lay in the dirt. Every hair on their bodies had been sucked off by the tornado.

Most people ran into their cellars as soon as they saw a tornado coming. But one young boy wasn't quite so lucky. He was sucked up into a tornado funnel. All his clothes, including his shoes, were torn off. He landed miles away, safe but stark naked.

Would you go to school?

Yes, but usually only for about four months in the winter. You had to work on the farm the rest of the year.

After you milked the cows and did your other morning chores, you'd walk to school, carrying your lunch pail. If you lived very far away, you couldn't go to school unless you had a horse or buggy. Often it was so cold, your feet and hands were numb and your lunch was frozen by the time you reached school. A pioneer girl named Nellie Warren kept warm by putting hot bricks in her buggy to keep her feet warm while she drove to school.

No matter how old you were, everyone was taught in the same classroom. You'd study reading, writing, spelling, geography, history, and math. Often, your teacher was a young woman who hadn't finished high school herself.

Most prairie schools had wooden benches, desks, and a blackboard — but no books! You had to bring whatever books you could find at home. Some students brought Bibles, some brought dictionaries or readers, so you hardly ever studied the same thing as the classmate sitting next to you. It wasn't until the 1870s that students were given the same textbooks, like McGuffey's Readers.

Spelling contests were a lot of fun. Each school had its own spelling team — much like a sports team. You visited other schools and cheered your team on. The pioneers so loved spelling contests, sometimes they'd get together in the evening and have one just for fun. You might even compete against your mom or dad!

What if you got caught in a blizzard?

You'd better look for a warm shelter — fast!

A prairie blizzard was no ordinary snowstorm. The wind howled. Often, ice covered your face, freezing your eyes shut unless you quickly wrapped something around your head. The blowing snow formed a white wall, so that you could see only a few feet ahead of you. People got lost and froze to death in their own backyards.

The worst blizzard was in 1888. It was called the school-children's blizzard because it began as children were starting to walk home from school. Some parents who went looking for their children got lost and died. But most of the children were saved, often by their teachers.

One teacher named Minnie Freeman became so famous that they wrote a song about her. It was called "Thirteen

Were Saved, or Nebraska's Fearless Maid." After the storm had blasted down the door and torn off Minnie's schoolhouse roof, she calmly tied her thirteen students together with a long rope so they wouldn't get lost. Then she led them safely through the raging storm to a house half a mile away. Another teacher saved her students by having them crawl into a big haystack.

To keep their farm animals from freezing to death, some people brought them into the houses. One man kept his pig, dog, four cows, and all his chickens in his house during a blizzard. They were crowded together in one room — along with his wife and six children. And they survived.

Did the pioneers ever need outside help?

The pioneers always helped one another. But once in a while, after a big disaster, they had to ask for help from people in the East and the government.

That's what happened in 1874 when grasshoppers ate all the crops. People almost starved to death. Many had no shoes or warm clothing for the winter.

When people in the East heard about this, they sent food and clothing to the pioneers. Everybody pitched in — church groups, aid societies, and state governments. Relatives sent barrels full of beans, bacon, flour, and clothing.

One woman helped collect 200 railroad cars full of food and clothing. The railroad companies transported everything free.

The U.S. government helped, too. President Ulysses S. Grant ordered the army to send food and 16,289 coats, 20,664 pairs of shoes, and 8,454 woolen blankets.

The pioneers got something else, too — seeds. Then they could plant their fields and gardens in the spring, and hope for a better year.

Who were the Exodusters?

After the Civil War, when slavery ended, blacks in the South hoped life would get better. But little changed. Some were beaten or killed, often by the men who once owned them. Many were cheated out of their crops.

In 1879, almost 40,000 blacks decided to head west. These pioneers were called Exodusters because, like the slaves' exodus from Egypt in the Bible, they, too, were seeking the promised land. Most of them headed for Kansas.

White southerners tried to stop them, because they didn't want to lose the cheap black labor. They beat up Exoduster organizers and closed the Mississippi River to boats carrying blacks. Armed men waited at river landings, looking for Exodusters. But nothing stopped them. Somehow they made their way west, many by walking.

The Exodusters who reached Kansas arrived with almost nothing but the clothes on their backs. But they found friends among the people in Kansas who had opposed slavery. More than $100,000 was raised to help the Exodusters get started. Money and food also came from Europe and the eastern part of the United States. Philip D. Armour sent money and beef from his Chicago meatpacking plant.

The first year, many Exodusters lived in dugouts, as other pioneers had done. But soon they, too, had their own sod houses and thriving farms. There were black communities all over the prairie. Nicodemus was the most famous black town. By 1888, it had several churches, stores, a school, and two newspapers.

The black pioneers also went to Wyoming, Oklahoma, Texas, Colorado, and other prairie states. They made up one of the largest migrations in the settlement of the West.

Did any of the pioneers give up?

Yes, some pioneers did give up and leave — usually because they were broke after grasshoppers or drought had ruined their crops. But many more stayed and refused to give up. They still believed that this was their great chance and that with hard work, each year would get better — which is exactly what happened.

The pioneers also liked many things about their new life on the prairie. Here people were always ready to help one another. And almost everyone started out poor, so no one felt inferior to anyone else.

Is there any prairie left today?

Yes, there are some places where you can still see the prairie. But most of it is gone. Instead there are fields of corn, wheat, and cattle, and towns and cities.

Something exciting is happening. The prairie is starting to come back! It turned out that some of the driest parts of the western prairie weren't very good for farming and ranching. Many people gave up and moved away.

As others leave, Indians are moving back to the reservations on the prairie. Instead of cattle, many are raising herds of buffalo. Cattle often die because of the freezing winds and deep snows. But the buffalo are right at home on the prairie. They can take care of themselves, because they are built to survive the cold. And they can feed themselves, too, even in deep snow. They just push their huge heads down through the snow to the grass below.

Also, private conservation groups are buying farms and ranches, then turning them back into wild prairie. And the U.S. government is working to bring back the prairie as well. But there is a problem: How do you bring back some of the special plants that used to grow there? Where do you find the seeds, when almost all of the old prairie is gone? This is where you have to be a detective.

Sometimes you have to look for patches of old prairie in the strangest places, like pioneer cemeteries or pieces of land along the railroad tracks. What may look like weeds are really treasures. Here scientists collect the seeds of the fringed orchids, shooting stars, and other plants that once covered the prairie. These seeds are planted. And little by little, the wild prairie is returning.

Visit the Prairie

Would you like to see what the prairie looked like long ago?
You can if you visit one of these places:

Thunder Basin National Grasslands
2250 E. Richards Street
Douglas, Wyoming 82633
(307) 358-4690
www.fs.fed.us/outernet/mrnf

Konza Prairie
Biological Station, Ackert Hall,
Kansas State University, Division of Biology
Manhattan, Kansas 66506
(785) 587-0381
www.ksu.edu/konza/keep

Oglala National Grassland
Nebraska National Forest
125 N. Main Street
Chadron, Nebraska 69337
(308) 432-0300

Badlands National Park
P.O. Box 6
Interior, South Dakota
(605) 433-5361
www.nps.gov/badl

Wichita Mountains Wildlife Refuge
Route 1, Box 448
Indiahoma, Oklahoma 73552
(580) 429-3222

Buffalo Gap National Grasslands
Visitor Center
P.O. Box 425
Wall, South Dakota 57790
(605) 279-2125

Grasslands National Park of Canada
P.O. Box 150, Val Marie
Saskatchewan, Canada SON 2T0
(306) 298-2257
www.parkscanada.gc.ca/grasslands